WHITE CITY

DISCARDED

White City

Poems by

MARK IRWIN

BOA Editions, Ltd. —— *Rochester, NY* 2000

LC #: 99-97274
ISBN: 1-880238-83-7 A paperback original

First Edition
00 01 02 03   7 6 5 4 3 2 1

Publications by BOA Editions, Ltd.—
a not-for-profit corporation under section 501 (c) (3)
of the United States Internal Revenue Code—
are made possible with the assistance of grants from
the Literature Program of the New York State Council on the Arts,
the Literature Program of the National Endowment for the Arts,
the Lannan Foundation, the Sonia Raiziss Giop Charitable Foundation,
the Eric Mathieu King Fund of The Academy of American Poets,
The Halcyon Hill Foundation, as well as from
the Mary S. Mulligan Charitable Trust, the County of Monroe, NY,
Towers Perrin, and from many individual supporters, including
Richard Garth & Mimi Hwang, Judy & Dane Gordon, Robert & Willy Hursh,
and Pat & Michael Wilder.

Cover Design: Lisa Mauro
Typesetting: Richard Foerster
Manufacturing: McNaughton & Gunn, Lithographers
BOA Logo: Mirko

BOA Editions, Ltd.
Steven Huff, Publisher
Richard Garth, Chair, Board of Directors
A. Poulin, Jr., President & Founder (1976–1996)
260 East Avenue
Rochester, NY 14604

www.boaeditions.org

TABLE OF CONTENTS

William Irwin 1927–1998

The way we had come was all we could see. . .
—John Ashbery

ONE

WHITE CITY

Shirtsleeved, walking out into the spring, occasionally
we glimpse a white city. We see it in the tiny lilies
belled within shade, and its taste, like gin or lemon, slightly
burns the tongue. Mushrooms drop their spores, while a faint
static mixed with song strays from open windows. Winter's unremembrance
is gone. Flowers walk among our hands. We do not know
which touch is which. Sunlight drizzles through green, and the magnolia's
thick vanilla scent makes the mind go numb. This dislocation
which feeling is. Distant, fossil-boned, the city
shines. We approach it in our dreams, or see at dusk its thousand
yellow windows hived. Toward it invisibly we move
the way flowers move toward sun. Desire moves
in our wings.—Rain then sunlight shivers through cloud
until it seems the paper houses might dissolve. Irises poise
to unfold. Pollen blows across the ground, and in our houses
a bright-seamed light leaks beneath doors. We move
and are moved by what shines, and there is a distance
forever vanishing between our bodies.

NO CONTINUING CITY

between two *whens* between
two *whens* man made a godflashthing

and the bees leaned deeply
into the flower. Please measure my weakness

with your power. What is
the half life of a moment? What beauty

is chance changing us
so quickly? More slowly, how sweetly

you blur the contours of my
body. The price of knowledge is

* * *

nature. And the quick jacket of light clothed everyone.
And the light was wedded
to the darkness. And the earth

was wedded to the sky. And the water
was wedded to the water. And the water
was wedded to the fire.

How dark into the far do the dead sail?

* * *

And the transom of light leapt to an ocean of shadow.

Pouring out over the bridges the knocking sound
of bodies.

        Pouring out over the bridges
the knocking sound of bodies.

              —Words
in a verbflash torn out of their mouths.

* * *

And Jisenji Temple that had vanished
And the unopened tin of mandarin oranges
And the black rice and the black trees and the black people.

* * *

"Thou still unravish'd" now
let the act begin now let the bees
hungry gold priests drowse with the sweet taste

of—. What is that "lowing
at the skies"? Now "Lead'st thou
that heifer" and push the tungstening bright

flash down over the land?

HORSE

On a metal table, a horse's heart and lungs.
I stare the slow miles down. July, the Rio

Grande's green tongue. Desert nights, crystal
animals, —a silver throw of stars. Constellations

stalked us: Love's incredible velocity
standing still. The left ventricle's giant balloon

still filled with blood: a rushing in my ears, wind
through juniper and sagebrush, on red rim

rock a clattering of hooves. *Will you, will you,*
I said. The coarse mane and straining neck,

the frantic whites of the eyes. The *Sangres,* snowy,
astonished us, as we were to each other, always close-

up & far away. The left ventricle courses fresh blood
throughout the horse's body. The right ventricle

sends blood to the ochreous lungs. Canyons sleep
in our straw hearts. Breathing is what saves

us. Anonymity lives in that rust-turreted land. We
made up new names, places without destination. I

once said *I love you.* Somewhere those words still
stand, a ruined adobe chimney. History changes easily

when people talk too much, or are simply struck
speechless. The skull's stark white light

frees us. Now I want to push my hands into each
of the heart's great cavities. My hands are heavy

& red with the earth. The horse is a great table
that holds and carries us over the land, selflessly.

MANSION OF HAPPINESS

People stand in front of a large white house giving
things away. June light floods the windows and occasionally
they look up as toward a familiar song. They stand on
the slow green hill of their lives. The air smells with rain
and the flowers are in want of their hands. They give
things away because their bodies are tired. Distant, a jet strays,
its tiny silver lozenge an impossible word. A woman says
"I remember Will" and a slight wind moves through the trees. Belief
is this language pulling them together, holding them
apart. The words need them so. Someone passes cookies
around on a silver tray. There are chairs everywhere
but no one is sitting down. How important it is to love
what is gone. Mary says "my son" and the word is handled
—clean and simple— like an egg peeled of its shell. Everywhere people
are whispering "I want you to have . . ." Detached from everything
they are open to all. Love's pollen flies. Dandelions spill
bright coins on the lawn. Shadows stretch out long. Trees pool
against sky, the pale joinery of clouds. A bird sings *how
long, how long*, while a boy listening to his Walkman, walks
down the road. Everyone turns and smiles. They watch him
watch the world. Soon they will go inside before the house is gone.

IT IS

now as the body begins to feel the light

shift and slow in August that I think of all the people

that love and have loved and suddenly I become

happy. I saw a street beautifully disfigured by rain

and a man dripping wet walk with no hurry.

He said, "There is nothing we can do that will save us

with our bodies." If only I had believed him,

and now, often I become saddened when I see the red smoke

people have left with their bodies. That desire

keeps us going. Now is a stream running in all directions.

Gather the water, for desire is written across air

and water, and I have watched sunlight on flesh turn to fire

beneath water, and I have watched moonlight on flesh turn to a darkness

one struggles to remember. Memory, that water

we still feel, the body's water, bodiless memory. I don't remember

her shoulders, but the smell of green tomatoes on my hands.

I called once, and the call was light and quick as a bird vanishing in dawn,

then I called again and it was like a man at dusk trying to lift a heavy

table. Love is not bodies but a smell of vanishing green.

ELK

That it was —fleshwarm, earthen, a marvelous
breathing thing. And the glance, a lastingness from cornea,
milky, asking sky. And if you had seen the great beast

fall —unsure, to its knees, then struggle the leaden head—
gaiting a few yards, before collapsing, antlers first, like a black oak's
crown, top-heavy into earth, you might worship the stubborn

gravity of land, and the garden, sudden its insides: Harvest
of soft, wet rocks, melons, —or is it a cave where the menses
of a secret ocean have dried? —Blood from the mouth. Tongue,

beard-black, says death. —And teeth, yellow seeds, from which all
these boulders grew? And here's the intestine's white chain mottled
brown, its lumen narrowing down like a perfect sentence

pronounced by God. And here's the great comma of each lung,
bellows undone. And here's the slug, a period in the heart's
balloon. And now this sunrise of flora and fauna

laid out, bloody map of the thing apart, and you
the hunter, instructionless, emptied of passion, crossing
green rivers, climbing red cliffs of meat, pulling off

the hide, walking out into another life, down the femur
to knuckly knee, you fall on the ground to worship
the bluestone and glass of each hoof, spoor lost

among root-sort. And now, shearing the meat from bone,
pulling the backstraps from spine, separating the loin,
hacking the fat from hide, whittling the pink from ribs, all

thirteen pair sculpting the air, jailing the light. —*Spirit out,*
spirit out. The head in a tree is a tree gazing toward
the wind-singing cage, toward the invisible bird of the heart.

TWO PANELS

AS WHEN

As when, flesh upon flesh, we tried to make our bodies
one. As when the sun blew orange-flamed music into clouds
that sang us from our bodies. As when the fire leapt with greed,
omniscient, wealthy in the dark, and we watched enviously
with fear. As when we thought we loved, but only made another body.
As when we walked far into the field at dusk and tried to see
where the eyes were, where the eyes on the skin of the snake were.

OR

a kind of silence only possible at night and far away. Or
what we can no longer discover out of doors and beyond.
Or late in autumn, the city's cavernous light and widening skirt
of shadow. Or over there, someone unpacking boxes, voices
to be sold before lost in the air. Or the enormous blanket of night
unfolding, and a faint, distant singing which suspends us. Or
the bloody stars of our teeth when we have spoken too much.

AND SO

someone gets an idea, or does something, or desire
turns rain into an ocean, and people either drown
in happiness or its absence, a kind of indifference,
the soil of these passing moments we live as the sheaves
of nights and days turn into chapters and a wind

blows, and glue cracks from the spine. If only we
could walk from these pages like characters on a road.
Instead, memory writes another line of cloud,
snow, or sunlight at dock's end, and you feel both sad
and happy, as in evening when things drift toward another world

you would like to follow but cannot, except in sleep, the swift
fluid of night collapsing all you did, snapping its black cloth,
inventing another day, lessening the whole, or just rearranging
the patterns of shadow, dream, where occasionally
a white dog waits and the hunger is yours. So you invent

new combinations of words, gluey with feelings
and memories where maybe the glow of a thing will
shiver, throw off a brightness like pollen others crawl
toward —pushing the lilac and hyacinth— greedy, clumsy
for more as twilight's gold syrup lies heavy on wings

still desperate for this world and its light, leaking everywhere,
fleshing the green. "Tomorrow we'll go to the park," she
says, then wakes twenty years later to rain, the red leaves
holding on to the sidewalk's window like cells of blood. We
need someone to constantly remind us, someone to whisper,

"Don't go away now, your daughter's freckles will be gone. Better
walk home today, you might glimpse a god, the toothless Chinese
man, stooped with crooked spine, who pisses by the dumpster

then laughs." The world is his —random at will— discovering
news among trash. Pray to him. Forget what you are, for you

are the answer to the question he asks while others
thumb through names in a phone book and an inevitable
gray wind hymns through the spines of numbers.
We keep building something the air takes apart.
There, steeped in blue, high above, a jet's silvery

needle is darning it shut, above this hotel where a man
and woman swim in a pool continually widening.
They swim toward each other but farther apart. The man
waves then slips off an invisible edge, his eyes
printed with soft explosions of cloud.

A NAP IN SPRING

The world continues without you, rooted
in sleep, a soul the future loves. Who are you
now, traveler, sucking a world's phosphor images up
through the straw of your brain while dicotyledonous
things remind you how we are all love's pawns
riding a wild green carnival watched by the violet
eye of some cloud. Impossible perfumes seduce
you: hyacinth, lily, iris, lifting their invisible skirts
toward a farther, more beautifully intangible sex. Trees
drop their yellow sperm across the lawns. People sneeze.
The soul leaps! Worms irrigate toward the sun. Insect
larvae shiver, swell, opening into the air's gown
and hungry orange beaks ravenous as gods. Dragonflies,
flame-blue, needle and mend the horizon. When you
wake you will be exactly between two worlds,
learning to let go, learning to hold.

THESE CARS

are the tired words around a city's great
walls. Mystery is speed. Listen, get

in. Beneath the dashboard's lamp
the map begins to resemble an animal's
insides. We breathe. The freeway

expands. Bodies of jets pass
low overhead, 1/2 spaceship 1/2
god. Civilization has stenciled our lives
so we might avoid that chaos

we crave. Nights with stars. You could hear
the cities dripping upward
toward their centers. That was before

the word had become motor. *Hurry
up, I can't hear you. Drive
faster.* The future

unspools and the dead grow closer
with each page of concrete
poured. But what

we are here for
must somehow be spoken
beyond where bridges make
a thwanging sense

of the land. *Shhh.* I'm whispering
faster, farther, disappearing
into less. I'm

saying I love you I'm
wrapping the word around
your body.

BUFFALO

They are the earth we have forgotten.
And the great continent of the head knows this
and will look right through you from the brown stones
of the eyes. And I would know them as a child knows
the brown-humped land that listens
for the prairie wind that is the bellows of their lungs.
A friend and I once stopped, astonished by the mile-long
herd, and by the slow train of the hooves
drumming up an expiring music like wind like God like sun.
Still I marvel as the late Nebraska light gilds the horns
and the ponderous mass of fur, while the foothills blue,
recalling the cold declining length of the rifle's bore.
They are the color of the earth thrust up, and history
still roams in the matted rags of hair, in the bleached litter
of bones, and in the chalky cliffs of the skull.

TWO

X

Because every thought is either memory or desire, the world

pulls away on both sides. Anyone's wish is a bird, and a wish

unfulfilled the unwinged skull, but a seed —fuzzy— pushes

its past toward tomorrow, all flutter and ecstasy. That's why

whenever I see people touch, I place a small white X where they

stood. Chalk, wind. Rock of sugar. Rock of salt. We spend our lives

licking at both. We sleep, eat, cry, sing. I like most when

it snows, when I must reinvent the shivering marvel of each

X, as knowledge is recollection, and love all discovery without delay.

DISCOVERY

Across the urban sky the slow bass sound
of jets, invisibly latticed, so many vibrating
strings. They are this century's music, a soft tearing
of air, a music of excoriation, a larger breathing

* * *

than us all. In gray November air, the museum's a dark canvas.
Outside, people pause and talk hesitantly
about real lives, too small or large

* * *

to be contained. Driving west in evening, in what seemed then
a larger dream, he stopped in a small mountain town.
Taking the map, the butcher traced
with sinewy fat and blood on his fingers
the fibrous sections of roads

* * *

through green. The grandmother dying, shrunken to half her weight,
looked out the sunny window of the nursing home
and said, "Look, there's our house." And the sad
thing was not the lack of recognition, as he held her bony
head up to the glass of water, and up to the aquarium's
larger glass walls, but that all of the houses looked

* * *

the same. Colorado, Wyoming, Utah. History
and freedom. The future of nature is dream.

* * *

The little girl's fingers all impatience
all over the silk bows of her presents. Mansion
of Happiness. April. The green hazel limb heavy
with the swarm's gluey gold. A kind
of fire in their bodies, inextinguishable because the queen
loves darkness. The words I heard after so much
breathing through cheap hotel walls in Kansas.
"You wouldn't have had to have had me,"

* * *

made me think that we are all divested travelers.—Space.
To what extent are astronauts dead men?
Or men trying fitfully to conceive? I kissed
Dorothy inside the Statue of Liberty. What a staid,
athletic pose. "Where are we going?"

she said. At the church everything was
conducted in the past. "Would you have taken
this man to be your . . ." "Yes, I would
have," she said. We left a little sad

* * *

but hopeful for that past. There is little as beautiful
as a bright yellow bulldozer
breaking into the dark earth
and moving it around like a big mechanical
sunflower shouting, grunting

* * *

some kind of love. The memory of being in someone's body
is not unlike remembering someone who has died.
What allows the physical to become bodiless

* * *

summons memory to replace desire. The suburbs
endlessly sprawl. They want to redeem us
but do not know how. I live
in a box with a window. There is a tree
I water on Sundays. No one ever

* * *

visits. When the hive swarms
the new piping queen is unlocked
to ensure the species.
All wing she loves

* * *

the darkness. The newspaper clipping said
he shot, but missed his sleeping wife.
"Just a bad dream," he confessed
to have said, soothing her back to sleep
before he shot and killed her

* * *

then later went to the movies. Imagine
having to imagine a wilderness,
unable to remember

* * *

one. Lewis and Clark reported a herd of buffalo
stretching farther than a man could

* * *

see. We live in a ravished world.
Once violence was real.

EVEN NOW

Still I try to remember when you first caught
fire, the barely visible flames about shoulders and arms
accentuating everything you touched, and I first saw
through words into their origins and hearts. I watched
you reach for a glass dissolving in air, while your
sight tore holes in an April world drowning
in rain and flowers. We walked through a park where
you stuck your hand in a young retriever's mouth, feeling
the hot pink gums and new teeth, while a little girl
wearing a ladybug cape swooped, singing over the grass
as bees droned *is, is* over the jonquils. We drove
to the country and walked through fields and meadows
and stood beneath an orchard's new gauze where you
talked of the past, picking chunks of time like invisible
fruit, and I could feel the rivers and trees engrave us.
We entered a half-built house, flooded with sky, and you
said, "There, there and there bodies will blossom."
I remember how it began to rain but you did not get
wet. How the fragrant wood smelled like a ripening fruit.
The sun came out as the evening grew long, and where
you lay down in the field to sleep there was only a red glow
resembling coals in a fire, a warmth I can feel, even now.

SPRING &

the seed shivers, upping its green
stars. We walk toward the observatory
witnessed from above. The moon knows all
this, taking pictures as we kiss. Knows the flowers,

cosmos and oxeye, volleying against
the gate. Knows what they
erase. Blue sky and clouds float across the cathedral
of your watch dial. One moment

you're gazing at the face of an infant, the next
over X rays not yours. A president waves, and keeps on waving
from a black limousine. We are present
in history, but we are

gone. The swan becomes visible in the Milky
Way and June brings freckles to
a daughter's nose. People line up to look
at the moon. I think it is the white light and shadow
they love. The caravan of bodies

continues to go on. In July along the Rio Grande
the volt-blue of the New Mexico sky
leans incandescently above green sage. We
keep on driving to forget. The river
keeps on remembering the land. "A Red

Giant is a fuel-depleted star
beginning to cool," I think the astronomer
says. In the middle of Lakeview Cemetery the Corps
of Engineers has built an enormous
dam. —"The Sea of Tranquility is the largest

shadow you can see." Joel Marcus took a close-up
I'll never forget: a handful of pink plastic
babies dropped on green
felt. Tiny arms and legs identically
agape. Some things

scare me. How on Sundays the paper houses
and people seem to shiver, ever so
slightly in their place, their
very breathing the continuum for light.

ANATOMY

We touch the skeleton of a nameless man. We touch
his bones and hear their names: clavicle, scapula, sternum.
I touch vertebrae of the spine and see the tree a boy climbed.
I touch caged ribs. I would strum a song he loved, watch him
frame a house. Did he have a wife? I can see her scream
flower. There is wind. Wisps of cloud streak by.
I touch hands that will not hold seeds but whose phalanges
could rake the earth. I touch his feet and watch him brush
snow from the steps of a house. Look, there are guests arriving
to eat, talk, sleep. I touch smooth ears of the pelvis where
still the sacrum would flower, listening for stars. I touch the skull: orbits
where the eyes were, where light, ravenous, roving, lived. I touch
holes of the nose and mouth and watch a man wipe milk
from the lips of a girl he will kiss, trusting the marvelous flesh.
The class has gone. Outside someone sings
and I feel everywhere the marvelous whiteness listening.

SERIOUS EARTH

A long metallic necklace of cars on an interchange
at dusk. —And then the noise starts again, and the crowd moves
toward the new stadium to watch what some think
games of darker-shadowed selves. O what they sing

and shout. In one tent a carefree, twelve-year-old girl
tries on her first bra, while in another a man twists
through the final elasticities of death. People grip their tickets,

moving from tent to tent. Look, there in the light
a great pile of spectacles. What men once looked through,
now only the sun finds, its final gold salve

a hymn too late. "Never mind the past," one sings.
"The future is a beautiful deliberate machine: us
it aims." *If, if, if.* Was it immutable truth

or cartoon?— The pavilion marked *City of Boys*
sounded like so many engines, but is filled
only with trees, a nursery of spruce and pine. And then the noise
starts again as a man and woman begin to embrace

outside by the gate. See how the hands and fleshneck
give way to the marble face, and then the kiss is frozen
and suddenly they wake, surprised as strangers, and join
the shoving, pushing crowds down Joy and down Misery

Streets toward the main event. Inside a nodding man
reads, reads in a dim light —while others listen and wait— reads
from old telephone books, their paper cities stacked high, walled
up like impossible gates: Chicago, Denver, Albuquerque, Salt

Lake. He reads in the unspace between hands
the tiny black bridges of print. He reads what is
and what once was with equal grace: the giantism of lives
reduced to shuffling names and numbers. He goes on reading
and they go on listening too late, waiting to be called, waiting not to sleep.

AUTUMNAL

The saffron-colored leaves are cresting into their moment. It's
the impinging lateness of things that's scary. Rusting,
rushing leaves now astonish, omitting what
they began to say. I saw people standing
in a circle on a hill, and the youthfulness of bodies
slowly began to separate toward soul. Perhaps forgetfulness
is a way of cleansing the far. I saw a woman
with yellow hands and red lips weave
through the circle. She spoke but one word and they
loved her. Their names were leaves in no
hurry. Her lips were the world's cherry. They said,
"Stop," then "Go faster," while the grapes' purpling scent
pierced the air and each brick of the old house
seemed an impossible slowly melting hour. I saw
the kite in the air. "The wind must be greater than the weight
of the string and its body." —Clouds, sun illumined
their marrow. The slow furiousness of leaves
blew at our feet. "Give it some string," he said, "and feel
how strong the pull." The man carried the kite
home. The leaves are nothing but words. How wonderful
it is to be here. And because we are not gone, still we are early.

THE MOVEMENT

We crawl, we eat. Like commas
we pause and curl
recalling the egg. Like 6s
we sex the dark.
We smell, we touch
though blind we crawl

* * *

toward light. From a lover
we hang a thread.
We fray, dissolve, and molt,
juicing the translucent
shell that hardens its
cuticle in air. My body's
tongue will dissolve

* * *

toward wing. I am
a key. The sky is a door
opening, opening
has no end. We are
in love with the earth
and believe me
a leaf will

* * *

leap. To wake up and find
you are in a holy place,
a place touched by someone
now gone, a ravishment
you will not wake from. The dream

* * *

of our bodies like the stars
goes off and on. How once outdoors
I saw you among trees disappear
with the swift shadow of a plane, but later found
your sleeping voice in a shell, your face
in a swirling return of cloud, its mansion of light
laying wings down gently over the land.

I HESITATED

before entering the body factory. I had heard
what happens when given eyes, arms, mouth. We
obsessed over occurrences of cloud. Unwillingly
we applauded the light. What would a nose? What
ears? What hands? What ecstasies a tongue
might trace? We leaned and pooled with evening.
We grew thirsty and slack. For what? I think
darkness urged us on, though some remained
ghost-smoke at the liminal track. I remember how
a bird sang something liquid I could taste as they
pulled a silver wire through my brain and the words
coughed into place and suddenly I wanted
everything the moments, the senses could fleece.

WIND

Like spring, the world continually rushes away. Do we
belong where we are going, or where we are? Hope
is not here, that huge invisible window we carry
and are afraid to set down. Perhaps the future never
really moves, but blows before us, a sheer white curtain
upon which fleeting images are screened. Like animals
we begin free, but unlike them we must decide, and each
time we do, some of that freedom leaves. The space wants
us more. Unlike them we are unable to hide. We build
houses, have kids, grow gardens. We are a spring frenzy,
a picture that scribblingly fills. But the frame seems
to push in more closely. How do we move beyond its lines?
unless our lives become a theater of spirit: Several people
locked in a room with ladder, several small windows,
and only the books they have written they read to themselves.
No one ever leaves, but each is unwittingly surprised
when the old man unlocks a door, just for her, just for him.
Clothed in dark garments we are creatures who by talking,
moving the words, gradually they gift us toward the invisible.
And why not? It was all we were ever worth.

ASKING

They asked a dying man if life was everything. He said
yes. They asked a young man if love was everything. He
said yes. "But we only live through love," they said. They
were like a cloud and spoke as though they'd been
here before. "Please," he said. "One more day, week,
year." I remember the happiness I felt when the knife-blade
slipped on my finger in the open field. —The smell
of blood, rain, earth. I saw the wild iris's sheer violet
silk in the late sunlight and I knew. I saw the cows
bowed to the wet earth and wild timothy, shagging the flames
of their tails, and I knew these things were true, outside,
beyond the moment the way the wings of the swallows blown
sheer gauze in the light seem beyond the sheer body of sky,
or how a place remembered with a friend is lifted beyond
all maps when that friend is gone. Memory is beautifully
static, and yet we move while life and its events arrive
lifted in a sudden wind, or are held there unnoticed, arranging
themselves into a bouquet. In this way eternities pass
until we are gone and happy and in want of nothing.

THREE

A WAY THE LIGHT WAS

How completely useless beauty
is, a window the gold light passes through, a door
we open and almost close. In April, just outside Del Norte
where the Rio Grande runs slow, I can't forget
the fresh-cut lumber stacked high, all buttery in late
evening sun. I kept leaving and turning around to the unbuilt

house and sounds of kids playing in the yard. What we
do not own is imperishable. What we desire
constantly beyond. The long slow *yes* of the Milky
Way, the red earth below. The cosmos all stare. And you think
of the time when time asks for your body, when the stars drop
their tiny white arrows into rock. The visible

* * *

is not real to the soul, moving as one moves
in a world of snow, knowing those white shapes
for content, invisible, not form, looking as one looks
through two windows of a house, and knowing that a room
exists between. To find that giving which goes beyond
and to learn to use words for what cannot

be said. Dawn's soda-white light, a porous
skin all over the Chalk Cliffs at Mt. Princeton. And as you
gaze the sudden sense that you are walking into
and out of your body, that its quiet skull is remembering
you. *Is desire Light? Is will Light?* And at what point does it turn

to darkness on the body? I remember Christian telling me
he loved her, over and over, pushing the words
into my eyes. And I remember Kelly holding the body
on the table, cold, lifting the slackness up, white
shadowing toward then, until all there was
was what we held, a singing light from paper, eros's slow

* * *

carnival come round. The body's lisps and groans, its clean
god-lusting sounds etched somewhere beyond in that shine
being is: Reyes flooding the fields, walking the Conejos
with his earth girl. Hay and manure smells, bawling
of calves and frogs, giant cottonwoods, the swarming
stars, mud, and the way the heat lightning made the houses

seem more real, till dawn and we slept, or dreamed
it all. Blanca Peak is not real, as seen from outside San
Luis, always close-up and faraway. That's why we
climbed it. That was real, but then we didn't care, looking
down, unable to pray. Reyes and I talked about this,
pushing the dead aspens down, —dusk, outside

Vallecito— collecting wood, while a flicker knocked
time out on a log, and the invisible hand of a giant
moved light, clouds. We felt so alive. And we both
knew what it was —a man, woman, the cabin half-built, a window
looking out on the place they'd never leave, and suddenly
those people became more than their lives, so close

to the changeless they could sense the moment shivering
into hours, days —sunlight, snowmelt, river-run,
jonquils and wild iris all over the still-flooded fields,
the frogs choiring some still life between childhood
and stars, while someone else stands on a city street, a casualty

* * *

of life, an accident without cause. The present is
all magic no one can untie, but perhaps glimpse, following
impulses of the land, impulses of the heart, which lead us
into another time, moving rapidly at first, like the river's lens
dirtied with silt, but slowly resolving into a stilled

ocean we can remember. The long slow *yes*
that beauty is, a mobile only occasionally brushed
by winds of similar lives once yours. Its skeletal
music, though faint, and barely audible at times,
does not stop but seems to come apart in that wind

you breathe. Mary Lou hangs clothes out to dry. Bill
washes the car, while Laura, all silver-haired in floppy
hat, carries fresh rhubarb up the hill, its pliant stalks
a fabulous late red in her arms. And then Hollis
walks beyond the garden one evening and asks

how they choose the dead. Spring is what being is.
When the earth is all seed-shiver and the air's a wet
gown, when millipedes and silverfish bristle along baseboards
and larvae gorge in the dark. The earth loves their sweet
jelly, loves the orange columns of ants, loves the bees'
slavish gold and the billion legs of grass. —Desire, shivering, makes

* * *

us forget. Something is flowering larger than us. Something
our contentment almost fills. It reads anniversaries
and engagements the way light reads trees vanishing
at dusk. And just when we forget everything we fill
it most, the way those trees grow large and more darkly
beautiful with dusk, and we move far beyond where

our bodies go. To wander is to love the far-chance-body
no one knows. Jefferson, Fairplay, Como, these ghost
towns dissolve like flesh on history's spine. Here, larkspur
and lupine gem a dry field, and there on that distant peak
snow melts more slowly than it falls. A veiled radiance
we almost see, light creased and jointed by cloud.

That's why you stare, that mountain what the waiting earth
makes easy, while our own cloud-bodies zoom
past fixed things. And so by traveling, ever moving, we
slow the process down, for what we touch and love moves
as we move, and like bees we travel from flower
to flower, drunk on a sweet fake radiance that pushes

home, the past, and that other darker thing away. The day
you first did it in the barn, it whispered in your
ear, and each night, rubbing your skin, rhythmically
against hers —proving to yourself you couldn't make it
vanish— you glimpsed, underneath, a river all evaporative

with light. Once, outside Alta Lakes, I watched Mary
watch the sun's last gold ribbon trunks of aspens.
She did not move. And then her hair and body
turned that same gold, and a bird flew into and out
of her body. And what was true was what did not move,
or what we couldn't see that sang. And then I could not reach

her with my hands. Inside this seed are fish, rivers, fields, trees,
a lover's hands, a tiny war, sun, rain, and a peaceful
day that in seconds passes in a year, the way a fish swims
quickly but forever against the stream, the way
a bird picks up a seed and carries a life away.

FREEWAY

The freeway, the finishing freeway unwilding the far. I
want to go. Headlights drift onto a dark sea. Rain:

Through its shivering lens the sky looks back: Oars beating
out rhythm toward a new world —green— all wild &

verb. *Go, go, go.* Sparrows dart through leaves, their wings
filtering raw light, air. Gills of mushrooms open, close. EXIT

HERE: The city's lights, clustering, illumine like fish roe
or stars thrown out on some lake's bottom floor. There's

an epic disguised among that coast of trees: Ships, bridges,
towers, once unbuilt, now collapse into celluloid. Light

burns their images once again. The highway as film we,
here, shivering, develop. The city as projector: REWIND,

PLAY. We planted a tree, but moved. *FLASH.* Is it
still there? *FLASH.* Before history there is geography,

after history there is fire. A child makes a white paper
box, pinholed at top, windowed at side. Through it

he glimpses a ghost-sun whose darkening period ignites,
burns across the small white paper like settlers moving

across a plain, until finally their desire extinguishes, borders,
halts. The METRO PHONE BOOK collapsed from its hook

is a ruined agora pushing back into earth. How vital it
once was for hands to touch. Names, numbers. First there

are names, then numbers, then the numbers become tired
of names and history has no one to find. Surveyors

are triangulating on a vacant field. Is the distance
between civilization and wilderness too great for the heart?

FLESH

of this world I live for— a woman you named
earth, a man you called flame. —Where are you
now? And who are we without these wolves we call
bodies? I remember in sunlight the webbed, half-
finished chrysalis shining on a log as a cloud
passed and a shadow, briefly, grew. And I remember
leaving, how I rubbed her body with a page of sunlight
whose every line I knew till she became a story
I could not enter. I remember the airports and train
stations, the rising and falling and encircling of arms
reminiscent of a field at sunset and the air's fresh
slaughter of wings. I remember and in remembering
begin to loft through the air, seeing the pollen, yellow,
everywhere in dusk and the colossal mouth of green,
growing, calling. I see our voiceprints on leaves losing
color and the precise lanes of our bodies moving
toward autumn where the animals stop, look, and say
once without speaking through the air's gauze of snow
where everything appears to be either angel or skull.

MEMORY

1.

I live in the lap of a mountain, a valley shadowed with pines
and the occasional clear word I trace upon
square after small square of snow. Where have the people
gone? Spring's yellow forsythia and white spirea
bloom and a stone church presses its quiet weight

into the earth. Please remember this: The deep
green bowl where with flour a thousand
times she dipped her hands, the jar of dried
apricots still leaking sun, the tiny scratches teeth
left on every spoon, —the sugar on the counter, and blink

2.

she's gone. Driving down the mountain we see the fossil-city's
million torches, flickering like the mind's, etching gold into
slate. So many buildings, houses remembering
lives, as the charcoal scar of that deer remembers, still trembling
on the wall at Lascaux? At San Ilfonso Pueblo an elder

keeps talking, keeps talking while a youth writes a perishing
language down, a language blushing sacred
mysteries as the sun's red vowel pushes mud kivas
back into the land. To ants that cow skull

is a mountain. To me it dreams of rock, cloud,
moons, and lilies soft as a heifer's tongue mooing
a wet calf up in April cold. Even now
wind reckons the jaw. Next door all summer

3.

a hammer's *tap tap* becomes a house. The world
is full of buildings which become broken walls, hearts
undone. A poem is a house of light
without walls, a child's language wandering
remembered by an old man. To be lost

is pure grace. I am holding that cow skull
now, tracing the intaglio line that one cell
dividing eventually made, feeling where the fascia
held the greater sheath of skin. Its shell bleaches
to the color of these mud walls where I am window

to this house. And now with magnifying glass
I am on my knees, by the door, studying
the tiny galaxy of scratches traced all around
the lock. Fossils, hieroglyphics, fool's
tracings, memory's arms grown marvelously
long, marvelously touching and weak.

RUINS

On a blank TV screen a tiny ship begins to appear. It has
been arriving for hundreds of years and carries tired
people to a new world. Joy, hope, fear, and desire
burn like an acorn's green fuse in their chests. The god
that drove them away welcomes them ashore. Tide-lash,

slick-rock, winter-sleet, and when there is sun the shadows

are long. By evening it is summer, a summer far
beyond. Within a white picket fence a mother
plays tag with her kids, and a boy NOT IT runs through
the twilight off the edge of the lawn. *Tommy? Where*

is Green Tom? A field mouse scurries away and that hawk

becomes plane. A bright-yellow bulldozer keeps grunting
along. In a field where a plow point was found
a drive-in now stands that few attend. Seen
from a distance the great screen resembles the moon
where shadowy figures occasionally pass, collapsing

history. Between summer fireworks and Christmas

lights, lives vanish and reappear. On TV an Indian
is selling pictures of fire. Each one is a little different.
They make you want to cry. I squint into the distance
of a city's ruins and try to remember where the river
was. Clouds, and beneath those clouds —animals, people,

trees, each leaf an atlas only the dumb heart can read.

GIVE

Floating along the tops of the Sangre de Cristos
the slow popcorn of clouds.
All day the summer wears us like an invisible gown
and the wind whispers *It is the outside*
you can never have, whispers this through the trees,
their great breathing lungs. Rivers flood.
The creek smells like a root

split open. Enter those
with nothing. Come in. At midnight
we flooded the field, stood in the oozing muck to dream
the hayfield brightening like fire. River me
with desire, —here, here, and here

we wade through stars, flesh to their
skeletal design. In the pitch-black a calf
bawls. To give is the future
tense of to have.

THE GRASSES

From a distance, when purpling clouds lean down close
        over the billowing green, the grass resembles a sea.

So many kinds of grass in meadow and field
        where we ran till dusk, till our lungs would ache

and we would fall down into the sweet deep sex. —Then a great
        darkness we never had time to go into. Ran and ran

                        * * *

till our parents called us away. So many kinds of grass
        —alfalfa, crested wheat, timothy, and brome. So many

vanishing cities: Berlin, Hiroshima, Baghdad. —Cumulus
        clouds rise like white temples over the fields

where we saw lovers and discovered the sounds
        they made. *Schhh, Schhh*, says the grass. I saw a wedding

in a field and the bride was the color of earth after
        rain, and the groom was the color of late-evening sun.

                        * * *

Spikelets and panicles arch, aflame with light, light
        shuddering across the grass. People run and time flares

during moments of joy. A blond wheel continues to turn
        and the dark one you never see. Sometimes the grass

is a bird, or lion asleep, and sometimes this field's a body,
        and when you breathe feathers spill from your mouth.

* * *

Picnics vanish and reappear in the sun. A snake braids
     and unbraids the earth. Evening, I glimpsed two children

dancing in the high grass, but when I got closer
     a woman and man held each other, young and glad

in the ancient light. One day Christopher walked into a field
     and never reappeared. His body was blond like the grass.

And where did Marie go, and Henry, and Tim? The wind
     knows, and knows how centuries become minutes

* * *

in a field. Breath, feather, chaff, germ. Sometimes
     the sky slips down invisibly through us and I think we

will never die. Where to? and how did we let them? and why?
     A woman with flour on her hands waves. —From dried

grasses a girl wove dolls. Their hair was gold yarrow. Their
     eyes were holes. She buried them among corn and we were

* * *

afraid. Dusk and the cows are brune leather statues,
     mouths sucking at the field. Above, the first stars are

hungry too. Sometimes at noon in August, the white field
     looks like paper on fire, and birds fly up like a people's

lost words. Say *grama* and feel a tiny wind sail beyond
     the word. Placed between your thumbs, a blade of grass

can make a song, a song of longing. We never knew
     what for. October now and the blond field's the color

* * *

of sky at dusk. Just gazing we feel in balance and in
       prayer. In the seedhead holy shudders of light remain

while the new bales stand like ruins of an impossible city
       we are too late to enter. Everything is dry, but wind

is water in a dry field, and the field is a sea. Look,
       we are setting forth. I'm speaking to you now,

whispering in a sheathed gold. Come, while the light leans
       and is going. —Breath, shadow-feather, cloud.

HUGELY

the world greens, opens, remembering. —What? That to keep
means nothing now, jonquils and mittens alike
tossed up from the plasm of snow. Sun now and then,
fast, hot. Clouds big and low
browse till rain, a musty scent that reminds
you to be dumb for a while. That wagon
more red on the lawn where violets jewel,
dwell, and dandelions, their scruffy heads fleece
the yellow air. Spring, when time is the time you're
conscious of. When *t'be* and *t'have* mean trembling
transitory things, a minutia, a yellow generosity
of pollen saying *call her*, *call him*, for what you desire
you will remember and make shiver
again. And blink go the vanishings —wing,
birdcall, petal— returning us to some common
world. And so you lie down to listen,
the billion legs of grass walking beneath a blue sky.

FOUR

THE WINDOW

that gives the light is not the window
to close, and it's this light falling
upon flesh that memory

knows. The glass of water in Christopher's hand
or the milk that Maria spilled
still shines, buoyant

as the last evening light touching
these houses, and you remember voices
you can no longer hear, until maybe the rain

walks through the trees, or the sunlight
walks through the rain. Faces, lips,
hands, over and over, knowingly

and unknowingly perform
beautiful accidents, an astonishment
the body finds.

THE SHEER WEIGHT OF HISTORY

lessens, as after years the weight of actions
lessens, becomes light as feathers, though their lessons
still the mind. The torturer's weapons recede into his name,
his name into the war's, its shadow lessened
by distance and by other shadows drizzling over

other names. It's almost as if we didn't listen
when the present fleshed the years with lives, when love
seemed possible and often was that eternity we
became bored with, and so acted out the *yes*
or *no*, or merely waited for someone else's

action. Now like innocence it's something past
losing: balloons rising, just out of reach
from the child's struggling hand that gradually becomes
a kind of helpless, happy wave? And so we look up

and back where history is a fat old man
who by telling stories to children gradually lightens
till all his weight is theirs, and suddenly
they are older. Was it thought that gradually

handed us over to becoming? As though some
child, ghosting up the rainy windows, drew figures till
the daydream blurred to action, and those actions
froze, drifting farther behind

his bearded hand. The stone chimney
still remains amid the vacant field, while discoveries,
declarations span the air like invisible bridges
or the fading contrails of jets we know

are there. Are they? We are the flame, history
the fabulous shadow where forms
no longer crumble, an eternity
made to measure what the shivering imperfect flesh

did. Names, deeds, numbers. More and more
we feel them lessen as we grow older, listening
more intently as the new snow falls, singing *once*,
always, lifting something up, covering the dark with feathers.

WORDS

Always departing, or waiting to arrive, as inclining, rapture
moves toward the light, and that the radiance always
comes from a distance, not close-up, where among blood
and grease we live, except for the few moments. I remember
how she would pick the orange cat up and, almost indistinguishable
because of the aura, hold it, the shining world in which they
were one. I would say *girl, cat, window,*

and feel the words, their tiny wind
falling away, frayed attempts at making the thing,
the light, its small time happen again. Once in a chapel's
muted light, I watched a man, woman, and priest
christen a child with a name long and numinous

as a cloud— Benjamin. The perfect hope
of it folded in and around his tiny body struggling
like a word, words that so quickly abandon us
or cling to our bodies like glue. —Or how, after Chris's
death, trying to talk the sadness, we could feel, taste our words
stir the slow syrupy air, or hang, skeletal, a fish's bones, blanched,
that would vanish with light or another's

laugh. Once among talus and daisies
we sat while peaks eluded us in clouds, and laughing, almost giddy
from the high air, named rocks with no forethought
save what rough acts their beauty dragged from our mouths —tigel,
cranus, azul, xlana —and felt for a moment the wide spaces
and small dangers they would attend. As now,

lightly penciling these words on the paper's
white field, then lifting their tiny veils, listening for
jagged, spurred sounds, a laddering hesitancy that holds,
glints, jewels, as the room and windows dim, still hoping
a few dark syllables might rise. Outside,
dusk-lit, the trees seem ancient with their epic wings.

SPARROW

There is something I must tell you. Slowly we are vanishing
as I speak. —Something like hunger, faintly

beginning to stir from far off. Something
out of darkness, bulb or root pushing against the rain's

tongue. *Shhh*, the half-deaf boy said. *GGGod*
is a sparrow. The mangled words fell out

as he pushed his nose against the spirea's white
blossom goldloud with bees. Among so many

wings, language seemed
a ruined kite. Push his bike in,

out of the rain? Or leave it there later
for the dripping sun? Spring whispers things to you

out of sync. Fleck of this, fleck of that. Cardinal, or tulip
path. —Lips! What? What you didn't

say to her in jamcellar, then barn. Light splintered
and shot through the slats. Her taste, salt

in the rain. Page after page of it. Now sing
the way the straw makes its little shout against green

till the fire eats it and the real joy begins to shine like the sun.

BRIEF HISTORY OF DESIRE

Anise, wild raspberry, trout.
Should I attempt the word
only after taking the thing

into my mouth? Steep wash
of talus and mud.
Beyond, a cumulus cloud
blossoms from

stone. God
is the river's green
tongue where a girl and boy
swim, then fuck

in the sun. Loose
talus and greasy
shale. Look, spirifers
and winged brachiopods 300

million years old. Last night on
TV I toured the cathedral
at Rheims, following the narrator
down gothic-arched aisles. How could
such choired effort

not sing? till —floating
through channels— I fixed upon
one black-suited man
fistfulling up boweled mud
from a shallowing pond
while his good hand's
wrist ticked an elegant gold time

over Holocaust ash. Lupine's
electric blue nods
among rock. How much
complete order costs. Wilderness
does not design, but designates

the heart. Bones and feet
of a mountain jay. The
viridescent head
once vectored through trees; its skull's
now a frail, but stationary
kite. Eros

is like that. Hans Castorp was a great
shipbuilder, but found his heart
in snow's ash. A city's concrete flowers
rise. I build houses out of cards
then go on

long hikes. History will
never stop, nor
love, nor this river
cease. Alders grow thick
in the sand. Once I read a book
called *The Evolution*

of Disease. Cocci, bacilli, and corkscrew
bacteria gradually alter their forms
until immune to past
vaccines. On the second cast
upstream, I hook a twelve-inch

German brown. How complex with age
love becomes. The river
takes the trout's quick
blood. Even

stone memories
become undone. Once
in this same spot, my daughter
picked a dandelion long
as a wand and blew a wealth of winged seeds

toward the sun. Dusk
and a first few stars, though the canyon
still exhales a deep
red light. The universe expands

like a balloon with spots. Stoneflies
rise and fall, sheer wing
and threaded leg. The carnivalish shine
of cities and bridges

subsides. Under a flat
wet rock, a nymph's larval casement slides
between something skeletal
and some thing not yet

made. A great blackwedded darkness
pushes down into green.
Above, a jillion

birthing stars, and it's
spontaneity, not purpose
I love.

LIGHT

I think it's light, that something moving beyond the moment,
the hour, or why else would it call faces, astonished
from their chairs, to gaze into evening's blue jar filling

with orange, and dark. My father always said we should paint
the faces of those gone with our hands dipped in
light, the way these clouds, lower now in autumn,

paint the ocher land and our faces with gray, and an orange
mirroring that slow fire we'll join, as the bees push
their dry river of gold toward a final cold

light. We wear the river's light on our hands, that other
river, all border, outside, beyond. Just look at that man
waving to his wife, the gluey light webbed about fingers

leaking toward hers, hers toward his, —a shivering frequency
that holds, wants to go on, the giving light of our hands,
haloing the object, the object that endures

after we are gone, its sugary-ghost-light breathing
back a visible world, allowing us to recognize
faces, hands, the blush on clouds, —apple, pear— all

that is moving away with the moment, hour, while
the light shimmers, embalms, translating desire toward memory,
and how that continues, will not dry up, stubborn, rivering beyond.

THE BARN

The spring after your death I enter here, opening
a door into the thick shade. April sun balloons one
south window swarming with flies, zinging the light
you can't have or are made of entirely. Cats, pigeons
warble the air's one cool shadow. Here are harness, reins,
and saddle. —Pitchfork, hoe, rakes among which one
spade's shiny tongue sings to all the darkness. —Coffee cans
filled with nails. —What builded sleep? What framed
nothing? Tires doze and turn invisibly in their black
circles. Cobwebs spangle a corner, and here's gasoline
in a jar that looks like iced tea. Will you
return, tall as fire to drink, talk about the cows
plodding mud you loved? And here's an old mattress
you could sleep on standing. Chicken feathers, stones,
manure. A swallow darts among rafters. —Seed bags,
empty bushel baskets, old dolls and abandoned toys. Wings
move the air and halved voices call. —From windows,
from doors. The way the barn is ours and earth's dark home.

A MAGIC MOUNTAIN

I think a cleaner light moves behind that farther
mountain where air seems untouched by human
form. We came here for a cure because our
bodies slave to fashion some disease that steals
the air we breathe, although much less so at these

altitudes where indistinguishable seasons blur
the habit of our days. Ah, the habits of our days
fall regularly as snow until one of us falls
in love, an easy thing to do among the dying
at this altitude. Sometimes I think desires

unfulfilled become our disease, and if we
find love, it beautifully wrecks the reason
of our days. Just yesterday I watched for hours
a young blond woman dine. Delicately she spooned
fire from a bowl. I wanted to touch

her hair, to kiss her, to feel that other
slower shivering, not from chill or fever, but slavishly
beyond all will, just like the snow that squalls
without warning, randomly, throughout the day, folding
our minds beyond the body toward dusk, clouds,

and sleep. One evening, after hours of skiing, I
watched dusky miles of light magnify all
rose to shiveringly collect the day's remains
in an icicle, its light a child's grail
licked to nothing. That night I dreamed the hotel's

black facade carried the faint X rays of our
bones like swans. They moved against night's
immeasurable tide toward a snowy shore
turned water by the touch of warm, living hands. I
woke shivering from cold. My nose began

to bleed, and I realized that it's only when
in love, or afraid, that we feel this colossal
illusion we are alive, that sensual passing
of events we call the moment, hour, day, which
here completely dissolves through snow's

blank window, allowing us to recall, and dream,
squinting at its farthest unlit stars, the future's
sugar, and also memory's, this snow that comes
and goes so easily: Winter to spring in a day, flowers
and lovers pushing their impossible beauty among

the dying, which reminds in summer— this
brief wild clamor we are on the lit side of grass.
We have discovered the flesh's relationship
to eternity is zero. What matter? These bodies
are inessential houses, and I want to ski the snow's
beyond, a slave, where desire balloons memory.

AS WE WONDER

at something its meaning dissolves.
What you forgot, staring into the wooded
mouth of a trout lily. And what you forgot to say
as the frogs hymned their glottal
slop and you kissed her
beneath stars. Rhododendron and azalea bloom. A bunch of cars
honk at a wedding. Your daughter is born. Birthdays
sift through the house like evening light through a window
the sun will not close. Ever
you hope. Ash paths of sparrows
dart among green. The houses grow. A voice speaks
then looks for a long time. Still you wonder, till the light
burns your name into the edges of cloud.

SOMEONE

is building an invisible city
before us. They work slowly at night while history
is forfeited in sleep, or during brief intervals
of day when we forget, or gaze out
windows. The city both is and is larger than our dreams
where some of us visit, carrying our hearts
like red lanterns, which from a distance resemble
a carnival of joy so resplendent and sunstruck
we revisit those white walls time and again,
casting against that world the rose landscape
of our bodies, what some call our lives,
until one spring, gazing perfectly at both flowers
and stars, we become the enormous hope of forgetting.

ACKNOWLEDGMENTS

The author would like to thank the editors of the following magazines and journals where many of these poems originally appeared:

American Letters & Commentary: "Hugely," "These Cars";

American Poetry Review: "Discovery";

The Amicus Journal: "Give";

Colorado Review: "Mansion of Happiness," "No Continuing City," "A Way the Light Was," "Wind";

Denver Quarterly: "A Nap in Spring," "Autumnal," "Memory," "Serious Earth," "White City," "Words";

The Journal: "Brief History of Desire," "Freeway";

The Kenyon Review: "Elk," "Horse";

Mid-American Review: "As We Wonder";

The Nation: "Buffalo";

New England Review: "A Magic Mountain" "Ruins," "Sparrow," "The Sheer Weight of History";

The North American Review: "Anatomy";

The Ohio Review: "Vista";

Orion: "Asking";

Sniper Logic: "Flesh," Wind";

TriQuarterly: "Even Now";

Willow Springs: "The Window."

"Autumnal" also appeared in *The Pushcart Prizes XXIII: Best of the Small Presses*, 1999.

ABOUT THE AUTHOR

Mark Irwin was born in Faribault, Minnesota, in 1953, and has lived throughout the United States and abroad in France and Italy. His poetry has appeared widely in many literary magazines including *Antaeus*, *American Poetry Review*, *The Atlantic*, *The Kenyon Review*, *The Paris Review*, *The Nation*, and *New England Review*. He has taught at a number of universities, including the University of Iowa, Ohio University, the University of Denver, and the University of Colorado. He is the author of three previous collections: *The Halo of Desire* (Galileo Press, 1987); *Against the Meanwhile: 3 Elegies* (Wesleyan University Press, 1988); and *Quick, Now, Always* (BOA Editions, Ltd., 1996). He has also translated two volumes of poetry. Recognition for his work includes a "Discovery"/*The Nation* Award, two Pushcart Prizes, National Endowment for the Arts and Ohio Arts Council Fellowships, a Fulbright Fellowship to Romania, and a Colorado Recognition for Literature Award. He lives with his family in Denver, and he spends part of each year on a wilderness ranch in southern Colorado.

BOA EDITIONS, LTD.
AMERICAN POETS CONTINUUM SERIES

Vol. 1   *The Fuhrer Bunker: A Cycle of Poems in Progress*
W. D. Snodgrass

Vol. 2   *She*
M. L. Rosenthal

Vol. 3   *Living With Distance*
Ralph J. Mills, Jr.

Vol. 4   *Not Just Any Death*
Michael Waters

Vol. 5   *That Was Then: New and Selected Poems*
Isabella Gardner

Vol. 6   *Things That Happen Where There Aren't Any People*
William Stafford

Vol. 7   *The Bridge of Change: Poems 1974–1980*
John Logan

Vol. 8   *Signatures*
Joseph Stroud

Vol. 9   *People Live Here: Selected Poems 1949–1983*
Louis Simpson

Vol. 10   *Yin*
Carolyn Kizer

Vol. 11   *Duhamel: Ideas of Order in Little Canada*
Bill Tremblay

Vol. 12   *Seeing It Was So*
Anthony Piccione

Vol. 13   *Hyam Plutzik: The Collected Poems*

Vol. 14   *Good Woman: Poems and a Memoir 1969–1980*
Lucille Clifton

Vol. 15   *Next: New Poems*
Lucille Clifton

Vol. 16   *Roxa: Voices of the Culver Family*
William B. Patrick

Vol. 17   *John Logan: The Collected Poems*

Vol. 18   *Isabella Gardner: The Collected Poems*

Vol. 19   *The Sunken Lightship*
Peter Makuck

Vol. 20   *The City in Which I Love You*
Li-Young Lee

Vol. 21   *Quilting: Poems 1987–1990*
Lucille Clifton

Vol. 22   *John Logan: The Collected Fiction*

Vol. 23   *Shenandoah and Other Verse Plays*
Delmore Schwartz

Vol. 24   *Nobody Lives on Arthur Godfrey Boulevard*
Gerald Costanzo

Vol. 25   *The Book of Names: New and Selected Poems*
Barton Sutter

Vol. 26   *Each in His Season*
W. D. Snodgrass

Vol. 27   *Wordworks: Poems Selected and New*
Richard Kostelanetz

Vol. 28   *What We Carry*
Dorianne Laux

Vol. 29   *Red Suitcase*
Naomi Shihab Nye

Vol. 30   *Song*
Brigit Pegeen Kelly

Vol. 31   *The Fuehrer Bunker: The Complete Cycle*
W. D. Snodgrass

Vol. 32   *For the Kingdom*
Anthony Piccione

Vol. 33   *The Quicken Tree*
Bill Knott

Vol. 34   *These Upraised Hands*
William B. Patrick

Vol. 35   *Crazy Horse in Stillness*
William Heyen